LITERATURE & WRITING WORKSHOP

EXPLORING
NATURE WRITING

SCHOLASTIC INC.

PERMISSIONS— "Sand" from COME WITH ME TO THE EDGE OF THE SEA by William M. Stephens. copyright © 1972 by William M. Stephens. Published by Julian Meesner, a division of Simonm & Schuster Inc. Reprinted by permission of Paramount Publishers Inc.

Excerpts from THE TREE by Judy Hindly. Copyright © 1990 by Judy Hindly. Published by Clarkson N. Potter, Inc. a Random House Company. Reprinted by permission of Random House Inc.

From THE BAT IN MY POCKET, copyright © 1992 by Amanda Lollar. Reprinted by permission of Capra Press.

ISBN 0-590-49541-0

CONTENTS

COME WITH ME TO THE EDGE OF THE SEA

by
William M. Stephens

Illustrated by
Eileen Hine

H ave you ever really *looked* at sand? How would you describe it? Is it like sugar? Like salt? Like dirt or mud? Like tiny rocks or pieces of glass?

In some ways, it's like each of those, isn't it? But at the same time, it isn't *exactly* like any of them.

The only thing sand is like is…sand! But sand is different on different beaches.

New England sand is mainly quartz crystals. These were formed during the Ice Ages by glaciers grinding through the eastern mountain ranges.

In the warm seas of southern Florida, the sand is mostly limestone—bits of sea shells, coral skeletons, and other remains from the bodies or shells of tropical marine animals.

California sand is light, powdered rock which has been worn away from seashore cliffs by wave action.

Many beaches in Oregon and Washington are composed of fine grained, green-gray sand formed from molten rock that ages ago seeped from the earth's hot interior.

In Hawaii, some beaches are white or pink coral sand. Others are dark brown or gray, and they are made of lava and ashes from volcanic eruptions.

Certain beaches in Australia are composed of "star sand." Each grain of sand is a miniature star, the skeleton of a one-celled animal known as a foram.

Most sand is older than America. Some grains have a history dating back many thousands of years. But some sand is young, perhaps younger than you. Is it possible to tell which grains are ancient and which are new? Here's a hint: Pieces of seashells are often quite young. They are made of calcium carbonate or lime and are much softer than the glassy crystals that make up most sand. Crystals of quartz and other hard minerals will last almost forever without wearing away.

Next time you visit a beach, take along a magnifying glass or hand lens and look at the sand. If you don't have a lens, look at the sand though a plastic bag filled with sea water. This will magnify things a little. While looking through the seawater, you may notice darting and wriggling creatures that are almost transparent. These are shrimp-like copepods, slender-arrowworms, one-celled creatures and other kinds of floating and drifting life called plankton.

Take home a pinch of sand in an envelope or plastic bag and spread it out on a sheet of plain paper. Look at the sand through a microscope or hand lens, and you will see that every grain is different. Usually the grains are many different colors, too.

Sand grains near the edge of the sea are often smaller than the grains high on the beach. This is because the wind has blown away most of the tiny grains from the high part of the beach. These grains are carried long distances, and they form the sand dunes behind the beach. When the wind blows hard, you can watch sand build up to the dune shape. Watch a little sand hill for some minutes, and you may notice grains of sand dancing up the slope and over the top. In this manner, the dune slowly moves across the beach.

The movement of large dunes is very slow, perhaps five or six inches a month. But over many years, the marching sands may cover up trees and even houses. Along some shores, dunes can be found thousands of feet from the sea. Many centuries were required for them to march so far.

Have you ever listened to sand? Put your ear down next to it. What are the different sounds? The roar of the sea... people talking and walking... the calls of seabirds... perhaps a passing airplane.

Do you hear any other sounds? Listen carefully. Try to tune out the sounds you don't want to hear. Listen to the sand itself. Do you hear soft, stirring noises? These sounds may be produced by beach fleas or sand

hoppers. These many-legged animals are about the size
of a grain of rice, and they resemble shrimp. Sand
hoppers live in tunnels that they dig in the sand.

Do you hear a louder sound, like rocks tumbling
down a slope? This sound may be caused by a ghost
crab cleaning out its burrow. Ghost crabs live in a long,
narrow tunnel that may reach down three or four feet,
all the way to the salt water that seeps beneath the
sand.

Do you hear any other sounds? A scraping or buzzing noise? Use your imagination and try to picture what kind of animal is making that sound. Stir the sand with your hand or foot and listen. How would you describe the sound? Is it like a cat purring? Or water being poured into a glass? Or the rustling of leaves? If you have good ears and the ability to concentrate, you might even hear plants growing. As the roots extend and shove sand out of the way, a definite sound is produced.

When the wind is strong, sand grains blown across the beach may make so much noise that you cannot hear the sounds in the sand. Sometimes, too, the noise made by people walking or the sound of waves hitting the shore is so loud that you can't hear the sand animals. So it's best to select a quiet spot for sand-listening.

What does the sand *smell* like? Pick up a double handful of sand and hold it up to your nose. Inhale deeply. Let the odors fill your mind. How would you describe the smell to a friend who had never been to the sea?

Now move to a different spot a few feet away, and smell the sand. Is the odor different?

If the sand is moist from the sea, it may smell like seaweed. If it contains a lot of little creatures, it may have a "fishy" odor. High on the beach, where the tide cannot reach, the sand may have a dry, fresh smell, like fallen leaves in October.

Now smell various objects. Cup both hands around a shell or rock and inhale deeply. Smell a handful of fresh seaweed. Compare it to the smell of dead seaweed. Smell the wind. Notice the smell of the spray when a wave breaks. Does the beach smell different at high tide and low tide? Smell your hands while they are dry, and then smell them after dipping them in seawater.

Put your face next to the dry sand. Do you feel the sun's heat reflecting from it? On a hot day, the surface of the sand may become so hot that almost no living creatures can survive on it for long. In the middle of a hot day, the sand's surface may be as hot as 130 degrees. At such a time, insects may dig down a few inches where the sun's heat is not so intense.

You may see a red-and-yellow wasp digging furiously in the hot sand. After digging for a few seconds, he may leap into the air and hover a few inches, like a helicopter. The air is cooler up there, as much as 25 degrees cooler. Then the wasp may dig again for a while before again rising to get cool. He may repeat this several times until the hole he is digging is deep enough to suit him. Then he may dive into it and cover himself up.

Later in the day, when dark shadows move over the dunes, the wasp will sense that the air is now cooler. He will dig his way out of the hole and fly away.

The world of sand is always shifting, always changing. Imagine living in a place that is never the same from one day to the next! The creatures that live in sand must be strong and hardy. They must be ready to change their habits, or way of life, at any time in order to adapt to new conditions.

THE TREE

by
Judy Hindley

Illustrated by
Freya Tanz

Apple
The Climbing Tree

for pies
for cider
for crunching
for dunking
for wooden spoons
for violins

for mosses
crochets
honey-bees
for spring
for scent
for climbing in

19

THE TREE

The wood of apple trees is loved by wood carvers, and is used in the scrolls of beautiful violins. But when it's old, the apple tree grows gnarled and twisted into knots like a drawing with hidden faces painted into it. Moss and lichen grow on its knobbly twigs, as thick as mittens.

If you crush and press an apple, the sugar in its juice quickly turns to bubbles, making cider. Sometimes, wasps get nearly drunk on fallen apples —perhaps the apples bubble into cider in the sun.

If you have an apple tree nearby you can watch its apples start to grow, from the tiny bulge at the end of a twig, when the blossom falls, to the big sweet lump that stubs your toes among the leaves and grass in autumn. There are so many kinds of apples in different shapes and colours—round, long, heart-shaped; shades of gold and yellow and green and white and crimson.

*P*lane
The Itchy-Ball Tree

dingly,
dangly,
itchy-ball tree
for green
for shade
in parks
and streets

spots
and blotches
going up,
leaves
in heaps
beneath
your feet

A plane tree grows new bark like a change of clothes— always peeling, patching and "dressing" itself. Its glossy leaves are easily washed by rain. These things protect it from the dirty city air—that's why you see it on so many city streets.

The plane has a seed-ball like a thistle, with the downy seeds pressed together in the center, and the tails sticking out in a prickly ball. They dangle from the trees all through the winter. Then, as they ripen, they explode! And the itchy seeds go flying.

Look for a slender, elegant tree with a mottled trunk, like a giraffe. Look for branches held out wide, draped with a flutter of leaves like pointy lace, leaves to scuffle through in autumn. And look for seed-balls hanging delicately from slim, bare twigs in winter. That's a plane tree.

B eech
The Gold and Silver Tree

big as a castle
cool as a cave
calm as a church

Its trunk is smooth and silver. Its small, crisp leaves turn golden in autumn. It is a kingly tree, so strong and calm, often planted as a hedge to shield more fragile trees.

It makes a cave of green in the summer, like a hollow of a wave. Flowers often nestle within its twisted roots in spring. The beechmast—nut-like fruits that fall in autumn—keeps away scrubby undergrowth.

Listen to the sound the wind makes in its leaves. Each kind of tree has its own sound—whispering, rustling, roaring, moaning. Some people know trees by their sounds. A big, old beech has a high, soft hiss like a wave as its foam curls round a rock. Listen...

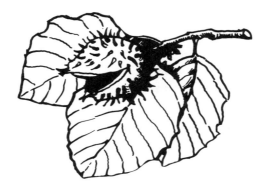

Horse Chestnut
The Conker Tree

conkers
in the autumn
candles
in the spring

THE TREE

In the spring, when the tree is bare, it is studded with big, golden bulbs, all pointing up, that seem to be covered with a sticky varnish. The buds are leaf-cases. Inside each is a tiny fan of baby leaves and, sometimes, the spike of a miniature flower. (If you put a budding branch in water, you can watch it open day by day.) As the leaves unfurl, the bud breaks open and out pops a limp umbrella of frilly leaves. Then, the leaves spread out like big hands, and the flower spike fattens and stretches and bursts into bloom, until the tree is covered with huge, fat candles of pink or white flowers.

In the autumn, when the flowers have withered, their spiky green fruits split open and scatter seeds—bigger than marbles, dark and smooth. For hundreds of years children have threaded these on strings to knock against one another, testing which cracks and which is stronger. This game is called "conkers", because of the sound the seeds make when they collide.

THE BAT IN MY POCKET

by
Amanda Lollar

Illustrated by
Jane Manning

The heat was oppressive the day Sunshine came into my life. I was busy creating a window display for the furniture store my mother and I have in downtown Mineral Wells, Texas, and had to interrupt my work to make a bank deposit. I stepped out into the hot sun with my mind still on the window display, paying little attention to my surroundings, and almost missed the small furry form on the sidewalk in front of the bank. On closer inspection, I recognized it was a bat.

My first reaction was a shudder of revulsion, but the poor thing was laying on its back, all fours in the air—obviously baking in the heat. Wondering if it was still alive, I nudged it with my foot; the disturbance caused the tiny creature to open its jaws and bare a mouth full of short, sharp teeth. The little animal was scarcely an inch and a half long, and I wondered if it really felt as

threatening as it tried to appear.

The bat wasn't pretty to behold, but it was definitely suffering. After gently scooting it onto a newspaper with the toe of my shoe, I went back to the store and found a box for the bat. Then, after filling a jar lid with water, I put the box in the storage room, where the bat could stay cool, and left it alone to die in peace.

The next day, much to my surprise, the bat was still alive. Assuming it must be hungry and not having a clue what to feed it, I tried apple slices, oats—even a dead roach, and left the offerings in the box. I checked repeatedly, but apparently it wasn't the right food, or else it was too sick or frightened to eat.

The second day found the creature still clinging to life. I

couldn't help admiring its determination to live, so I decided to do my best to help it survive, and took it home with me. Then, I went to the library in search of information to get this little bat well and on its way. I checked out the only available book on bats. What I learned that day about bats literally changed my life.

It turned out that I had found a female Mexican free-tailed bat; her diet mainly consisted of flying insects— such as moths and mosqui-toes. Relieved that she was relatively harmless, but still leery, I avoided touching her. Instead, I examined her by moving her gently around with Q-tips and discovered she had an injured wing. She was so weak by then that she hardly resisted, and I realized she needed food as soon as possible.

According to the book, a good diet in captivity was a mixture of equal parts of cream cheese, hard boiled egg yolk, ripe banana, crushed mealworms and a few drops of small animal vitamins. My cupboards held none of the ingredients. No eggs, no banana, definitely no mealworms— whatever they were. All I came up with was some banana nut bread and some cream cheese. After mixing the two together, I offered it to her on the end of a toothpick. She responded immediately and ate it up. Feeling

encouraged, I put a glob of the
mixture in front of her. She just sat
there looking at it, making me
wonder what to do next.

I consulted the book again.
According to the author, she would
have to be hand-fed. Reluctantly, I
picked her up, surprised that she felt
so soft and velvety.

Though she seemed reluctant to be
handled, she quickly gobbled up the
food I offered. This time she spared
me her teeth-baring routine. We soon
settled into a comfortable position
for both of us—her lower jaw resting
on the tip of my thumb with my
fingers cupped around her back, so
she was sitting straight up in my
hand. Her little feet straddled and
gripped my thumb somewhat like a
monkey. She had five toes on each
foot and a face that was rather cute
at eye level. Her lips were extremely
fat with vertical wrinkles and her
eyes were small in proportion to the
rest of her face. She had a pig-shaped
nose and huge ears with potato chip-
like ridges completely lining the

insides. In my fascination with her face, I didn't watch as closely as I should have while feeding her and, needless to say, food had spilled all over her lips, down her chin and onto her chest.

After she ate her fill, she started slinging her head to shake off the food clinging to her. This accomplished nothing but to spread the food up around her ears and on top of her head. I decided to try my luck with an eyedropper full of water. It was hard to tell when she swallowed, and she wasn't sure how to drink from an eyedropper, so now water was all over her along with the spilled food. By the time it was all over, we were both completely stressed out. With relief, I put this sticky, gooey, wet thing that no longer resembled a bat back in the box. Now she looked more like a piece of banana nut bread with feet.

While reading the book, I became more and more fascinated with bats. It seemed just about everything I thought I knew about bats wasn't true at all. Of all the thousand or more species of bats, about seventy percent of them eat bugs. Only three tenths of a percent are vampire bats—limited to South America—and the rest are nectar and fruit eaters. Just one insectivorous bat can eat up to 600 mosquitoes in an hour, and one large colony of Mexican free-tailed bats in Texas can eat a quarter of a million pounds of insects every night. Fruit and nectar-eating bats are among the most important seed dispersers and pollinators of tropical rain forest trees and other plants. Their food includes bananas, dates, figs, avocados, mangoes, peaches, cloves and more.

Contrary to popular belief, bats are neither filthy nor likely to transmit diseases. They groom themselves

constantly—even more than a cat—
and simply cannot stand to be dirty.
The poor bat I'd found must have
thought I was out to torture her
instead of feed her.

Most people believe bats are blind,
while in truth they see quite well.
Furthermore, they are equipped with
a built-in sonar system as
sophisticated as anything man has
ever invented. They are able to
detect obstacles as fine as a thread in
total darkness, so it's unlikely they
would ever get tangled in your hair.

Bats seldom have rabies. Fewer
than half of one percent of bats
contract rabies, and even those
rarely become aggressive. In the
early 1950s, researchers made some
mistakes about bats. Several bats in
these studies had rabies-like symp-
toms, but did not die. From this they
gathered that bats were unaffected
by rabies and could contract and
carry the disease over a widespread
area, because they would not die of
it. It was eventually discovered that
the bats they examined had a Rio

Bravo type of virus, which isn't harmful to bats or people, but is fatal to mice. The researchers had tested their theory by injecting mice with the bat virus, which, of course, killed them and started the rumor that bats carry rabies.

Another fallacy is that bats only like cold, dark places. They do prefer darkness, but still enjoy the sun's warmth. To think I had put the creature I'd found in the coldest place in the store and tried to feed it roaches!

Another interesting note is that bats aren't related to mice or rodents at all. They are of their own order— *Chiroptera,* meaning hand-wing. Bats are actually more closely related to humans than they are to mice. Earlier studies have had them linked to primates—which makes them our distant cousins. Upon learning that bit of information, I began to look at the little bat with newfound respect.

Intent on making her as comfortable as possible, I lined a box with burlap, cut ears off some fuzzy,

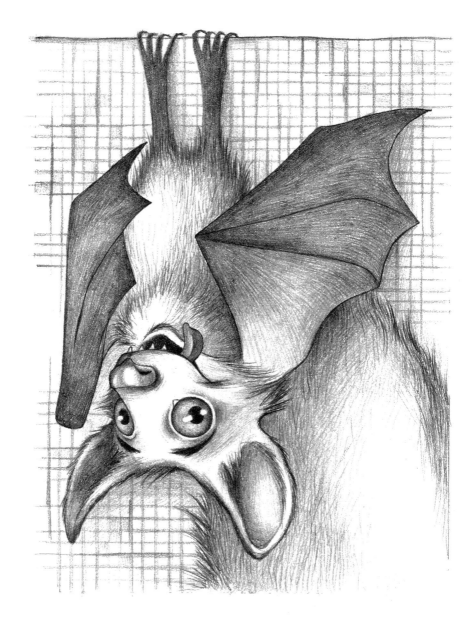

stuffed animals and sewed them to the sides of the box to simulate bats and, hopefully, make her feel more at home.

She seemed much more comfortable and found a spot right away beside one of the ears. Almost immediately, she started grooming herself—hanging upside down with one foot and combing her fur with the other foot. In no time at all, she looked like a bat again!

Assuming indoor lighting would confuse her nocturnal habits, I placed the box in front of a window so the sun could stream through half of it. With one box flap covering half of the open top and an Afghan placed over the entire box, the sun could filter through, and she still had a dark place to retire for sleeping. She would be able to see the sun go down in the evening and come up each day to keep her body clock right.

Now the bat had everything except a name. Since she was so opposite of everything I had first believed of her, I decided to call her Sunshine.

Now the problem was mealworms. What are they? Where do they come from? How could I get some? Off to the library I went again. Not much information was available, though I found a photo of one. I called my father to ask if he'd noticed any in an old feed barn he no longer used. Grabbing the box with Sunshine in it, I went over so my dad and I could look for mealworms together.

Luck was on our side. We found

quite a few in some old feed sacks with leftover feed in them.

Persistence paid off, and we ended up finding about two thousand all together; enough to last the whole winter, if necessary. My father offered one to Sunshine, and she ate greedily. Her face actually took on an expression of utter ecstasy.

Now armed with everything I could find to give her the nutrition her little body needed, I headed back home to make her next meal. As I was driving, I couldn't help but think about how her tiny body had all the same organs as ours—a tiny brain, heart, liver—everything is essentially the same—even the bones in a bat's wings resemble elongated webbed hands. I wondered if her tiny brain feared what her fate might be, and wished I could somehow communicate to her that I only wanted to help.

In order to keep Sunshine in good health, the mealworms would have to be healthy. The book advised keeping them in a big container full of

Wheatena with sliced potatoes for moisture. The laundry room seemed a good place to keep them.

Since I couldn't stand seeing anything suffer, I had a major obstacle to overcome in feeding these living things to Sunshine. It literally sickened me to watch her eat one alive. For days I tried various ways of killing them instantly but nothing worked. They still squirmed in agony and left me so queasy I couldn't eat dinner. Finally, I came up with the idea to freeze them, then thaw them out under running water when needed.

Sunshine's meals became easier. She seemed to enjoy them much more than the first meal, although she still ended up with a face full of food. At least she would inadvertently eat even more later when she cleaned herself up. She sure was cute when she ate.

At first I only handled her when feeding, but one evening, curiosity urged me into trying to know her better. We both still cringed a little

47

when I touched her or picked her up, but the initial fear was gone. Talking to her softly and saying her name, I stroked her small head with my fingertip to see if she would relax. I couldn't help but feel sorry for her, being confined to a cardboard box when she normally had the entire nighttime sky for a playground. And instead of other bats for company, all she had was me—a "giant".

Her wing injury didn't look too serious. A scab was forming on what would be the forearm part of the wing, but that was all I could see so far. The library book stated that any serious break to a bat's wings would cause the bat to go into shock and die rapidly, so I felt sure it wasn't broken anywhere.

Hopefully, it wouldn't take her long to fly again. Mexican free-tail bats migrate for the winter months, which were coming soon. If Sunshine wasn't able to fly by then, I'd be stuck with her for the winter.

Studying her closely, I was amazed at how she was put together. Her face was almost dog-like, but it showed intelligence like a monkey's. She was so borderline ugly she was cute. With fat little lips and a perpetual grin, she came closer to the resemblance of a troll doll than anything I had ever seen.

Her wings folded up tight and looked like long arms at her sides, extending forward towards her head with a thumb attached at the end. The thumbs were used for climbing and holding onto buildings. Along with her five long toes for gripping, she could climb as well as a monkey. When she walked, she looked like a little crab. All in all, she resembled about five different animals, depending on the angle from which you looked at her.

She seemed to relax somewhat as she sat in the palm of my hand. I stroked her tiny head and then continued with my finger on down her back. She didn't seem to mind, and after a few strokes, her tail started arching up a little more with each touch until it came up each time, much like a cat's when you pet it. I continued petting her head and then rested my finger in front of her nose so she could get used to me further. Her next move left me stunned. She sniffed my fingertip, then moved towards me and laid her wing across the end of my finger in a gesture that seemed to mean acceptance. I tried to find another reason for her action but her move was too purposeful to be anything else. Her small gesture filled me with awe and touched an inner part of me permanently.

It was now very hard to leave Sunshine alone. Each evening, I would get her back out of her box and hold her in the palm of my hand. Eventually, she decided she'd be more comfortable upside down and would turn so her head faced my little

finger and her toes gripped my first finger, with her little back against my palm. She seemed to enjoy being like this and would soon drift off to sleep. After a few weeks, she seemed to consider my left hand hers. I must have done the same thing subconsciously, because each evening found me doing more and more things with one hand.

At times when both my hands were needed, I could either put her on my shoulder or tuck her into the folds of my sweater and set her on the couch. She loved to look around while perched on my shoulder and would open her mouth slightly, sending off echolocation noises. Most sounds are undetectable to human ears, but every once in a while, a slight clicking could be heard. Children's ears are much more sensitive than adults and some can hear the noises bats make. In fact, some of the higher-pitched squeaks from bats can be painful to a child's ears.

When in the folds of the sweater, she would snuggle back with just her face and ears peeking out, looking completely content. From the couch, she could see me in the kitchen and would watch my actions unblinkingly.

I could easily keep an eye on her as well. Eventually, she would tire and just lay her little head down— lowering her ears down over her

eyes like a miniature sombrero- and
go to sleep. She reminded me of a
baby with a blanket pulled up over
its shoulders.

One day I made her a tiny blanket
just for fun. Setting her on a big
throw pillow on the couch, I spread
the blanket over her. Apparently she
didn't feel as secure as she did in the
folds of my sweater because she
didn't stay put. Finally, she went a
little too far and took a tumble off the
side of the pillow. Somehow the
blanket ended up beneath her. Not
being able to grab hold of anything,
she clung tightly to the blanket with
all fours. Down the side of the pillow
she rolled, all her limbs stiff in the air
and holding the blanket taut until she
was a fast little blur of blanket, bat,
blanket, bat, blanket, bat. Even
though she was headed towards the
couch cushion, I quickly rushed to
her aid. Picking up her trembling
body I tried to calm her through my
laughter. Needless to say, she never
drew comfort from her little blanket.

The weather was now turning

colder and I needed to wear the sweater Sunshine seemed to adore. A replacement she would trust was needed. Using an old black sweatshirt, I made a small rectangular pillow and stuffed it with cotton batting. I then folded the pillow in half and sewed the sides shut, leaving one end open. The whole thing was slightly smaller than a shoebox and resembled a dark fuzzy cave inside. She could go to the back and hide completely if she wanted to, or peer out the opening in the front and still feel secure. Since she was used to being in close contact to bats while roosting, the soft walls surrounding her seemed to give her comfort. I dubbed this invention her "nerf cave."

This book was set in Cheltenham

and composed by Marjorie Campolongo.

It was printed on 50 lb. Finch Opaque.

Title page illustration by Linda Graves

Editor: Deborah Jerome-Cohen

Design: Patricia Isaza